MASTERY OF SELF

The Foundation for Success
and Much More

Combines eBook Titles
"Mastery of Self - an inquiry"
and
"Mastery of Self - a closer look"

W. Dutchak

= Published August 2014 by W. Dutchak =

MASTERY OF SELF
The Foundation for Success
and Much More

Combines eBook Titles

"Mastery of Self - an inquiry"
and
"Mastery of Self - a closer look"

~.~

Also by W. Dutchak

Watching Thought
Thoughts and Time

----------------- ~.~ -----------------

ISBN: 978-0-9937862-3-5

DEDICATION

This book is dedicated to those who have begun to seriously question their relationship to life. The first little booklet "Mastery of Self – an inquiry" which was published as an eBook, is Section 1 of the current book.

Section 2 of this book was published as the eBook title "Mastery of Self - a closer look".
The first book (Section 1) opened the door to this inward investigation of life. Both sections serve the function of a device to set one on their quest of discovery.

Section 2, entitled "Mastery of Self - a closer look", expounds more detail in various directions so that one might begin to move aside the veils that block or shade clear seeing into the essence upon which human nature is based.

I invite you to share that which came through me in moments of stillness.

September 2014
wDutchak
St. Thomas, Ontario, Canada

--- ~.~ ---

CONTENTS
Mastery of Self - an inquiry
- Section 1 -

CONTENTS
Mastery of Self - a closer look
- Section 2 -

Wladicus

~~~~~~~~~~~~~~~~~~~~~~~~~~~~~~

- Section 1 -

MASTERY of SELF
- an inquiry

~~~~~~~~~~~~~~~~~~~~~~~~~~~~~~

1. <u>A Radical View</u>
<u>of Personal Development</u>

The term "Personal Development" has been around for a while. I suppose most people have a general idea of what it refers to. Very technical definitions turn most people off, since they do not really care what it means, but what it can do for them.

Often the term "Personal Development" is used quite loosely. Then there are various facets of PD such as building specific skills like:

- communicating via public speaking
- conveying ideas clearly through writing
- improving one's character traits to interact with more appeal in the "business world"
- overcoming some personal inhibition - relating to others with an open mind
- learning how to present ideas from an appealing perspective
- etc.

Material such as how to become rich or how do to things better do not really fall under basic personal development.

These are more in the category of how to sell an idea.

It can be part of the activity one brings into one's personal development, but in themselves, the "how to"s do not actually develop a person, they merely 'add to' their knowledge base.

There might be some side effects in terms of developing character traits, or having more material to draw on in speeches etc.

Can you see anything more here?

The radical view on personal development that came to mind goes something like this:

What if we were to understand personal development as an unveiling and enhancement of who we are?

Let's look at it from another perspective - .

Who are we?

-at the core-in depth

-at the heart

-in essence?

We have been conditioned by environment, by circumstances, by society, to believe and accept our life situation in a certain way. That conditioning is always at the root of how we function in our relationship with the world (people, ideas, everything).

Can we unveil, uncover, gain an understanding to see beyond those conditioned limitations that affect our activity and performance in daily life?

Instead of chasing "cure-alls", methods, formulas and the 'X' steps to success (which may work for a time, for some), can we see the truth of what our potential actually is?

If there is a natural ability or talent within us, how will we find it or 'see' it?

And then, how could we develop or enhance it?

-------~.~-------

2. <u>Personal Development</u>

(The discovery and enhancement of who we are!)

Are you waiting for someone else to define who you are?

Or, are you ready for the quest of discovering who you are?

Introspection, self-inquiry, relentless pursuit of the truth of oneself.

These are all key elements of the radical view of personal development.

And then what will you find?
Will there be a sweetness to life that
escapes one in the pursuit and
struggle for such things as:

"success as the world defines it"?
or "making your mark"?
or to become "a somebody"?

You already are a somebody!

What do you really know of the powerful depth of being that is you?

4

Who will define you?
Who will discover your true potential?

You can look to others for examples, but in the end, you must see your place in the task of personal development.

It will not happen without your insight, without giving yourself over totally to finding out what the truth of yourself is.

What is personal development?*** Who are you?

Is the answer out there, or, is it already available to you but you are not aware of it?

Why does one try to achieve something, anything, beyond the necessary things in life?

When is enough, enough?

Why do people feel that it is important to compare oneself to anything or anybody?

- one's standing in life
- one's abilities
- one's income
- one's wealth or lack of it

- one's health or lack of it
- one's good fortune or lack of it

Why should it even matter?

If Personal Development has any importance or meaning at all then it is in the direction of helping one to see your own misunderstandings, shortcomings, and how they relate to others, and life.

So it all boils down to "Who are you"?

Not the "defined", conditioned you. That, you have to realize before you can proceed any further.

But, who are you beyond the obvious?

If Personal Development interests you at all, then the above questions must not escape your careful attention.

---~.~---

3. <u>Who is "the Person"?</u>

Personal Development as the name suggests is all about the **development of the person.**

What actually is " the Person "?

> Is it something totally different from what or who you really are?

> Is the Person the image that you THINK you are? (In essence a dream image) - An image that is carefully built up by societal conditioning, desires, habits and fears...

Have you seriously made this critical self-inquiry, as have many renowned sages over the ages and seekers of truth, even to this very day. Those that seek to find that ultimate truth are likely less than 1% of the world. They do not seek to display their discovery, they live it as an example for those who have "eyes to see" and "ears to hear".

Person-hood may merely be the entry point of the evolution of the human being.

---~.~---

4. **Regarding Self discovery**

Is there such a thing as a "Personal Problem" or is it really that the "Person" is the problem?

This has relevant meaning only in reference to "self" discovery...

---~.~---

5. **The ROOT of Personal Development**

You ARE – I AM – S/he IS – BEING …

These are all different grammatical forms of the verb

TO BE.

> The forms/words all look different, they sound different, but they all derive from and carry the meaning of TO BE.

> **You exist** – You know this instinctively

> – You say "I AM", "I exist".

Your "BEINGness" is thus self-evident. There is no other way to prove it but subjectively. Objective science cannot point to your KNOWINGness that you exist, and that you thus declare "I AM" as do the 7 Billion-plus people on this planet.

I AM is the common name of every human being.

When asked who you are, usually, inevitably, you begin your answer with "I AM" followed by your name, or your title, or your position etc. : But the "I AM" is the common part with which everyone identifies themselves.

Is this "I AM" the 'person' or the "BEING"?

As we have noted above, following the grammatical logic "I AM" is equivalent to "BEING", but it is usually confused with the 'little me', the person or personality, the mental construct, the conceptual or worldly identity.

Personal Development is for enhancing the "worldly" I am this, or that, or something, or somebody. I do this, I like that, I will become better, richer, kinder, etc...

That is phase one in the conscious awareness of Personal Development.

Phase two moves one a step beyond

personal development.

The 'Person' is recognized for the role it plays, for what it is as a functional entity in the complex of human society. Then it is understood where the "Person's" place is in the scheme of what people usually call life. Addressing the factor of "BEINGness", the second part of HUMAN **BEING** comes next. This is part of the RADICAL (root) understanding of Personal Development.

---~.~---

6. <u>Regarding Human Being</u>

Human ***BEING***

- Phase III -

*** <u>Being</u> playing the Human role ***

---~.~---

7. <u>Regarding Certainty</u>

Can anyone say with indubitable certainty that their experiencing of the so-called objective world is not a projection of their subjective state of consciousness?

How do you think this might relate to "personal" development?

---~.~---

8. <u>Regarding Kindness</u>

Kindness is the natural state of true being.

It is native to all Life which evolves in harmony.

As human beings, we define this state of cooperation, helpfulness and good feelings in terms that makes all of us feel happy and secure.

Basically, what everyone wants is to feel secure, happy, and loved.

When you demonstrate by your actions that there is no intent to harm or attack another, you are creating an atmosphere of security and good feelings in which both can "shine" and be "lifted up". This is kindness in action.

We are all of the human "kind" and of Life "kind". Thus in our experience of Life what can be very naturally expressed is "kind"ness.

---~.~---

9. **A Good Place to start:**

IF YOU ARE NEW to this field of Personal Development then -

One instructive WAY to begin

your journey of personal development

is by reading Dale Carnegie's

stimulating "Eye Opener" book

"How To Win Friends And Influence People"

It just may reveal a new way of looking at the world and view relationship from a different perspective.

---~.~---

10.

<u>Regarding Deepening the Inquiry into self.</u>

Step #1*: Who Are You?*

The FIRST step is to find out WHO YOU ARE!

Then it will become clearer whether it is PARTICULAR PERSONAL HABITS or "the world out there" that is creating your "personal" problems.

---~.~---

11. <u>Mastery of Self</u>

When you begin to understand who you really are then the next step is to pursue the Mastery of self.

The ancient Chinese Master Lao-tzu, in his "Book of the Way" ... "Tao Te Ching" (pronounced Dow Deh Jing) pointed to many 'secrets' of Mastery of self.

One of them is found in the following Quote:

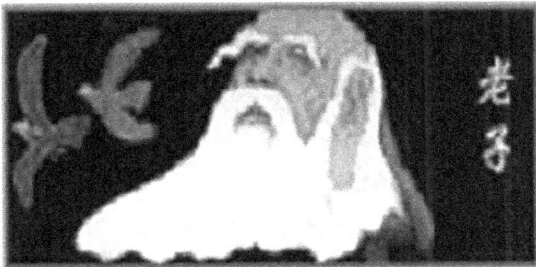

**Knowing others is intelligence;
knowing yourself is true wisdom.
Mastering others is strength;
mastering yourself is true power.**

The initial steps to Mastery involve watching thought.

---~.~---

12. <u>Regarding Watching Thought</u>

Have you ever watched thought?
Have you seen its character?
What is it in essence?

Is there freedom from
the limitations of thought?

Where is thinking most practical?
In what situations can thought interfere
with, and complicate your life?

As you begin to observe without being attached to your observation, you start to become an impersonal WITNESS to the activity of thought. With practice, a whole dimension of the phenomenal activity of thought energy unfolds to your newly focused awareness.

Now you are on the verge of true self-empowerment. With vigilant alertness, attend to the activity of thought without being caught up in the stories that it carries. Every thought tries to lure you by implying "This is important", or "Pay attention", or "If you don't do this or that, what will they think of you?", and so on, and so on, and so on.

These kind of interfering thoughts have no power over you ...

UNLESS you give them the power to rule your desires ...

What will you do?

Will you rise above all of this mundane conditioning?

Will you attend to the Mastery of self?

Do not delay to begin your journey of personal development ...

and BEYOND!

---~.~---

13. <u>Regarding Beyond the 'person'...</u>

Mastery of self

is the beginning of a journey

that goes far beyond

the current understanding

of personal development.

... It is beyond the "person".

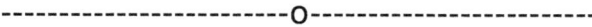

-------------------------o-------------------------

14. <u>Commentary on Truth</u>
Just some thoughts
Do These Thoughts Clarify Anything for you?

TRUTH is beyond thought and belief. It is totally independent of what one may think of it and it cannot be USED, or abused by anyone for any reason.

When truth is finally accepted as self-evident it is because the resistive activity of fixed, conditioned thinking has finally succumbed under the pressure of the evidence facing it.

Thought in that case finds itself incapable of doing anything constructive until it finally accepts the truth facing it as inevitable.

Truth is not something of the market place to be bought or sold or to be haggled over. It is the inescapable "**isness**" of the moment. Words fail to describe it adequately.

Do not bring TRUTH into Personal Development. Personal development is a game of "hope" invented by the ego, and a clever sales pitch designed by image building peddlers that take advantage of that human weakness.

The pioneers of "self improvement" did not peddle ideas in the manner that has become so commonplace in recent times. Those pioneers only hoped to wake up others to the wealth that exists within each of us, if we would only awaken to it.

Modern day "personal improvement" peddlers have made a sales game of it, and the human greed "for more", "for better and bigger", has made their job easy. They peddle everything from 'the improved body, love life, etc." to "how to become powerful and rich". This is preying on people's hopes and desires and capitalizing on their fears.

Would it not be advantageous to help people find out why they are prone to think and behave the way they do, and why do they not see it? Could this not help to improve the "human condition"? Can people be pointed to discover who and what they truly are, as opposed to who or what they 'think' they are, or what others tell them to believe about themselves.

Simply telling people what we think is good for them and how they should go about achieving our personal idea of "relative truth" in any area of human experience surely falls short bringing true self-empowerment to fruition.

How many people have pondered this with some real seriousness? I know that a few have done so, and the change has been dramatic and charismatic.

I have made some strong statements here, but I challenge anyone to source that very intelligence that makes life possible and see for themselves what the true human weakness is. For how awake is a human that claims to have the personal power to do anything, and at the same time blindly forgets the grace of the intelligence that manifests life, and makes what he or she thinks possible? This is, of course, the way that I see it.

---~.~---

15. <u>Mastery of Self is a Prerequisite</u>

Most people have no interest at all in meaningful self-inquiry. As for success, there are as many definitions as people who pursue it; but they fail to notice that any meaningful understanding of success, or its particular manifestations in one's experience of life has a prerequisite ---> The **Mastery of Self** and all that this Mastery entails.

---~.~---

16. <u>Self-Inquiry</u>

... no-one else can do it for you...

What is deemed to be perhaps a meaningful understanding of success?

This must be investigated in the light of careful personal discernment. One has to approach this with greater seriousness than one's beliefs and opinions:

Then **'meaningful'** has the proper context and only for the person in self-inquiry mode.

---~.~---

17. **The Soul?**

Many people question what this is, or whether such a thing exists at all.

Regarding 'soul':

1) this is obviously a concept as are all words

2) this can be taken as a metaphor pointing to a greater depth of our being.

3) Not knowing in this case is a bonus. So many people **assume** they know something just because they have accepted what others have said. This really stagnates one's learning process and inhibits the **Mastery of Self**.

---~.~---

26

18. <u>Developing What?</u> (A Game of Illusion)

What gets DEVELOPED
in PERSONAL DEVELOPMENT?

Have you considered this with some depth of understanding?

What is a "person" ?
Are you just a "person",
or are you much, much
more than that limited persona?

An entire psychology has been developed and promulgated over a very long time, and we have fallen under its spell, believing that we are only bodies and brains and the result of electrochemical reactions and synaptic impulses.

What a limited and limiting view! There is much more to the reality of being than the little, but ensnaring cogitations of limited mind. Consciousness precedes all of this.

You can discover this for yourself experientially.

<u>Mastery of Self</u> gets beyond this game of illusion.

----

19. <u>**Abiding in Awareness of Being**</u>

There is sometimes confusion as to what constitutes Mastery of self. Sometimes we see martial arts masters performing very fluent and rhythmic physical movements. We do not know if the particular person displaying those movements also has Mastery of self, but certainly we can see mastery of physical movement. Also in sporting events of all sorts, Mastery of Physical Movement, and perhaps the Mastery of mental concentration or one-pointed-ness is evident in the execution of the complex movements performed.

Performances by Olympic figure skaters is another example of great physical accomplishment. We cannot tell from just watching them whether there demonstrated skills proceed from the Mastery of Self in the way that I have explained it. It is still possible to accomplish great feats of various sorts without ever having Mastery of Self. One could be a great financial wizard, or a great salesperson, or a marvelous athlete and still suffer the various ailments of a limited, conditioned mind. Mastery of Self leads to total freedom of the illusions and delusions of mind.

Although many people associate physical, or intellectual accomplishments with Mastery of self, it is not that. It is merely accomplishment. Mastery of Self does not pursue accomplishment, although accomplishment is often the natural result of true Mastery of self. (Read the *Tao Te Ching* for more on this).

Mastery of Self involves the total mastery over mind, which includes freedom from attachment to opinions, desires; not doing things with ulterior motives in mind, and not pursuing results with specific outcomes in mind. In essence Mastery of Self is freedom from the concept of little old 'me' and my needs, and opinions and all the baggage that comes with being conditioned by limiting thoughts, beliefs and concepts.

Mastery of Self is the road of self-realization. In other words it is for those who genuinely seek the truth of who or what they really are, which corrects the misconceptions created by "THINKING" or believing who they are. It is not for the timid, or the opinionated, or the lackadaisical.

The personal self is a product of mind. In the Mastery of self one recognizes this subtle manifestation. A "personal self" identifies with mind and so the mind becomes master over self.

For one who abides in the awareness of being the mind is a tool not the master.

----

20. <u>Limitations</u>

The past exists only as we look at it now.

When the future arrives it will also be now.

By watching thought,

I discovered my limitations.

----

21. <u>Innate Intelligence...</u>

It has been my experience that everyday **IS** new, and there is really NO need to start anything because everything that is right for you becomes available to you to work out through innate intelligence. Just tune in, be sensitive to every moment of Life.

All potential and possibility lays there, at your disposal. Ah, but to be able to enter this mode of supreme creativity requires one basic attitude - humility, along with an understanding of what surrender to Life means. Then, words will never be sufficient to describe or explain your joy.

If you can see that, then you do not have to make up your own "thing to do" (which is full of effort for a very specific reason). This is part of **MASTERY of self.**

---~.~---

22. <u>Beyond SUCCESS!</u>

Is leadership a matter of control over others, or influence over others? Control is obviously not leadership. A careful inquiry into the nature of control will disclose that it is the result of fear. If one thinks that one has 'control' over others and then discovers that others do not see it the same way then the fear of powerlessness takes over and the potential for reactionary dilemmas and chaos is imminent.

Suddenly the conceptual leader is no more.

What about leading by influence?

One way that someone can have "influence" over another person is if the other person accepts proposed ideas as of value to themselves and thus **decides** to follow the lead of the person making the proposal. In other words, if someone identifies with the thinking of another then they have agreed to become followers of thought and consequently dis-empower potential intuitive leaps of creativity that may be superior to the ideas being proposed by others.

There are many 'levels' and 'shades' of perception to the business of effective leadership. Sometimes the most effective leadership might be demonstrated through silence (i.e. Non-verbal suggestion).

Once we have unveiled the inhibitions to perceiving "who or what we are" in *essence*, beyond all   mental concepts of self, –

> then we have begun the journey
> BEYOND PERSONAL DEVELOPMENT.

Personal Development might be considered the kindergarten of evolution towards greater awareness. It is not that we actually 'grow' to greater awareness for awareness is already total and complete, but we are inhibited from experiencing that totality and completeness because of conditioning by limiting concepts. Who we 'think' we are, the mind, is incapable of that uninhibited, awareness.

Self-awareness education (as one might call it), can begin when one realizes that the pursuit of "personal development" leads only to a 'dead end' in a 'blind alley'.

The understanding of self and one's

relationship to the universe (which includes people and everything), is the curriculum of the evolution of self. One might describe it as the awakening of the "higher Self", but let's not get caught in concepts now, for that prevents one from perception beyond the limitations of the conceptual mind.

Is this the road to success?

The great interest in *success* is the questioning of the conceptual mind. If you wish, you might think of the evolution in awareness as a subtle form of success, but that is still totally in the domain of mental conception and does not at all apply to the evolution of awareness.

Please note that:

Mastery of Self

is NOT a Personality Technique !!!

---~.~---

23. <u>Personal gain as motivator</u>

Whatever you set out to do, if you are empowered to do so, never do it at the expense of someone else.

If you do anything for personal gain then its value truly amounts to nothing,
for what is the good of your gain if no-one else can share or benefit by it.

No-one is an island; no-one can exist separate from the world, because everyone is an integral part of Life.

---~.~---

24. <u>What about TIME ?</u>

By stating or assuming that the existence of time is a reality makes it so in the belief system of the mind. 'Time' actually manifests IN YOUR MIND as a mentally perceived reality.

The mind is simply thoughts and thought-feelings. Remove those thoughts and there is no mind. Mind is just a word we use for the appearance of thought.

Another way to put it is that mind is defined by its content. The content of mind is simply thought, therefore mind is nothing more than thought and all things associated with thought.

We can state what we have in mind (i.e. our thoughts) without the need for any understanding of the concept of time at all. However, because we perceive events and thoughts sequentially, this implies to us that one thing happens after another, and we come up with a concept of time to explain that. Then we believe there is time, and thoughts take on a "life" of their own in that context of time.

If we identify with our thinking then we in essence "buy into" the idea of time and start to treat it as a reality in what we then call "our daily existence".

So, there is no need to state that time exists in order to speak your mind.

---~.~---

25. <u>Funky Phases</u>

Life offers many funky phases.
We would like to make it better...
Our instinct seems to be to push against,
to resist that which appears to have
invaded our 'personal order' as we
understand Life.

But perhaps it is not a mistake that various
challenges are offered
in our experience of Life.

Perhaps it is not Life doing it "to us"...
But perhaps it is Life doing it "for us",
offering us a challenge
to break through
to the next level?

In our presence,
in the only moment that ever is, NOW,
we can witness the actuality,
the all-embracing totality of Life,
and the love that is ever present
and one with us.

Perhaps we are the most intimate
with that Life
and it is not separate from us.

Perhaps we ARE Life
on a grand adventure of experience
through personality.

Perhaps…

---~.~---

26. <u>Regarding Laughter</u>

*Laughter is closer to who you really are
than what or who you think you are!*

---oOo---

Approach every person, adult or child, as someone of value. Be genuine and respectful in your interaction with another. Do not feel burdened by "personal" problems, nor show evidence of such when conversing with another person. Smile freely.

Other than genuine physical dangers, there is nothing really serious in one's life experiences. The mind always makes things appear to be more serious than they really are. It is a matter of attitude. Understanding this can help you find out who you really are!

... and ...

Punctuate your experience with laughter often!

27. **<u>A Pointer for Personal Growth</u>**

People all over the world
are basically the same in essence.

Just about everyone has habits and ideas
that someone else doesn't like or
cannot stand.

> Some people display characters that
> do not at all appeal to some of us.

It is <u>understandable</u> to be in disagreement with another person's ideas, or to deplore the habits or character they display to the world:

However, it is not conducive to one's own evolution to attack the "person" because of their apparent shortcomings, or our own "personal" dislikes.

<u>MASTERY of SELF</u> is the beginning of true success.

---~.~---

28. *The Master's Way*

From the "Tao Te Ching"
(Pronounced -> Dow Deh Jing)

Without opening the door,
you can open your heart to the world.
Without looking out your window,
you can see the essence of the Tao.

The more you know,
the less you understand.

The Master arrives without leaving,
sees the light without looking,
achieves without doing a thing.

---~.~---

29. <u>Illusion of Happiness</u>

There is happiness and there is the illusion of happiness.

Happiness is your true state of being when the "personal actor" aspect known as 'self', or 'I', or 'me', or 'mine' is not displaying itself in the context of a personal agenda of fulfillment, or personal gain of any sort.

Because our life experience is that of a transient world where things come and go and do not last forever, the personal kind of happiness is an illusion that lasts for a while and then fades. It is like the "person" who is here for a while and then is no more. The egoic self then yearns to recapture those moments of "happiness" that made the "actor" feel good, and perhaps imagine they were moments of "heaven".

True happiness is of the impersonal nature. When there is no "person", no actor, no egoic self, no personal investment in the outcome of projected hopes and desires, then there is fulfillment, completeness and joy.

However, the egoic self can never understand this, because it has a vested interest in things like survival of the imagined 'self', acquisition, perceptions of separateness from the rest of the world, as well as many other personal sorts of limitation. It 'lives' a totally conceptual life - "in the head", divorced from a holistic awareness of universal reality.

The first step to greater awareness is to be still and simply watch thought.

Watch thought as it moves and manifests as egoic fears and desires, likes and dislikes, opinions and **judgments, boasting and timidness, and all manner of "scripts" of reactionary, conditioned behavior.**

Mastery of Self is understanding the limitations of the personal and stepping beyond those limitations.

Therein lays true success and the greatest experience of abundance - the wealth that is one's true inheritance.

This is the source and substance of true happiness.

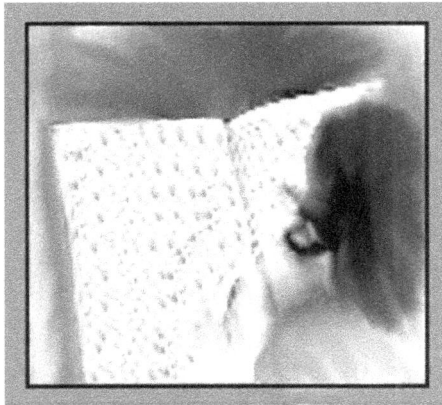

- wladicus 2014.04.26

---~.~---

Me and the Moon

Me and the moon -
On a warm summer day.
I look up and see that familiar crescent
In a sky that is powdery blue;
'Tis a summer sky, a warm and hazy sky.

Yet there she is – the lunar crescent:
Standing like a tilted dome in the sky.
Yes, 'tis the middle of the day
And that heavenly globe
Reveals a sliver of her mystery.
Anyone who cares to raise their
Gaze to the heavens
Is pleasantly surprised.

Patches of green lawn starkly stand out
From the ever-present ribbons
Of paved road and driveways.
Magically, a robin alights
On the bare tree limb
A mere meter away – and flies off –
Startled to have come so close
To a seemingly silent human.
For me and the moon 'tis a delight.

Like a guardian angel
She makes her monthly journey
Around this globe –
Bringing a bit of heaven to earth –
Especially in the dark of the night
When she glows in all her glory
Reflecting the majesty of life
Embodied in our star Sol.

Me and the moon –
An adventure in being.
It has traveled a bit –
I notice this as I take another peek
At that so-blue cloudless sky.

The music of summer
is vibrating in the silent spaces
Between the noises of mechanisms and
thought;

And that heavenly sphere moves on in silence.
In silent stillness it advances,
spanning the space of life.

Here I sit in wonder,
the moon and me.

-wladicus 2013.07.14

= END OF SECTION 1 =

===============================

~~~~~~~~~~~~~~~~~~~~~~~~~~~~~~~~

- Section 2 -

MASTERY of SELF
- a closer look

~~~~~~~~~~~~~~~~~~~~~~~~~~~~~~~~

1. <u>SUCCESS – Not many see this way</u>

When we pursue something called "Personal Development" we are referring specifically to the development of something related to the "Person".

To be successful in such a venture you must understand "what IS this PERSON that you wish to "develop?"

First look at the environment and the society in which this "person" is operating or manifesting.

Then address several of the main aspects that will have a relationship to the person's interaction with that environment and society.

What are this person's traits and can they be assimilated usefully into social interaction?

This will determine your ability to discern your value in interacting with your particular environment which includes the economic and social aspects.

- ✓ Are there changes needed to the traits of this person you will be "developing"?

- ✓ What would be the best way to address this aspect of "Personal Development?

Have a careful look at the environment to which you must relate harmoniously.

(Please note that "environment" refers to everything 'around' you, including other people).

- ✓ What are this person's strength's?

- ✓ Do you see a perceived asset to the environment in which you will be participating?

- ✓ Are there specific things relating to skills

that require your attention?

- ✓ Are there specific personal habit improvements or changes that you could make to improve your contributing potential?

These are only the beginning steps that must be considered if you seriously intend to develop this "person" that you have in mind.

It is important to note that you are NOT the "person". One might say that you are the "driving force and power" behind the person. The person is the "actor", the puppet, one might say; but only you have the power to develop this person into a useful contributor of whatever world environment you choose.

This is the beginning of the road to success. This is also the basics of self development in the sense of "self realization" and the "Mastery of Self."

Success is not something you acquire.

It is not a goal that you achieve.

Success is the ongoing process of being a useful contributor.

Success is what you make of yourself and how others see you in relation to their needs.

**Success is who you are in essence.
Your success manifests as fulfillment.**

This fulfillment can take any form (worldly, spiritual or both) depending on one's level of understanding and appreciation of life.

One of the keys to success is "giving", or being of service (to others or to life in general).

The more that you give meaningfully, the more "space" you create within yourself for the flow of life's abundance in various forms, to come your way.

This is really the basic understanding of the so-called "LAW OF ATTRACTION."

SUCCESS – _YOU_ – THE FORCE BEHIND IT ALL

Not many see it this way.

---~.~---

2. Be The Difference !

Personal Development can be looked upon as a game to be enjoyed. There *is* *no winner and no loser, only evolving consciousness.*

> What is this world filled with people and things?

> Why do some get ahead and others "drop out"?

= Be a "player" in this game! =

BE a meaningful contribution.

You can make yourself and others feel better!

Really feel better and not in the 'mind' only.

Participation in this game of "Mastery of Self" is not a mental practice. It demands your full commitment as consciously evolving life!

BE the difference. Don't just think about it.

You set the example, you become the hero. You don't do it for the results, they will come on their own.

Do you do it at all? Or is it done through you?

It is your <u>INTENTION</u> that sets the course of action and manifests the results that you call "MY LIFE".

----

3. <u>Will You Rise Above the Storm?</u>

A key aspect of "Mastery of self" is the realization that you are not the thoughts that appear to demand your undivided attention.

Conceptual thinking (reasoning) is a useful tool for survival and management of your everyday worldly affairs.

However, when the focus of the mind (thinking) is set on the "Person" (i.e. personal image) that you think you are, and the various associated emotional conundrums that appear to "rule your life", then that is the "time of troubles" that seem to plague us.

This is one area where one has to discern the "truth" in the game of personal development.

Everything is <u>experienced</u>
in the mind
(i.e. Thoughts).

Physically we may "<u>go through</u>" (i.e. Experience) events, however the actual "experiencing" occurs only in the mind.

The mind (thinking) conceptualizes (i.e. Translates) the physical events into various images which are stored in memory for later recall, thus giving the impression of passage of time and the "movement of life" so to speak.

That which is stored in memory is always "colored" by particular individual conditioning, beliefs, and impressions, so that the record created by mental processes is rarely faithful to the actuality of the experience.

Discerning the relative truth of experiential situations versus emotional memories of those events is one of the strengths of a "Master of self".

---~.~---

4. <u>A New You</u>

After you've developed the "Person"

(as per Personal Development)

then <u>WHAT NEXT</u>?

Have you tested the "new you" out in the world?

Have you noticed any significant changes to your personality (this relates to 'person')?

Are you still reacting in old ways to the thoughts that 'flit' across the mind?

Do thoughts no longer linger as they used to, creating unnecessary concern and stress?

These are just a few of the signs to look out for on your journey to Mastery of self.

The American professor psychologist Ram Das (Richard Alpert, partner of Timothy Leary of LSD fame) made a poignant statement many years ago –

> **"If you think you are enlightened then go live with your parents for a week."**

That should quickly clear up any misconceptions of whether there has been any real 'growth' in your mastery, or if it is just the 'run of the mill' kind of Personal Development – which is often quite illusory, self gratifying and short-lived.

Why short-lived?

> Because any 'surface' work on the 'person/personality' cannot meet the test of time.

There will be some situation, sometime, that will challenge "who you think you are" to such a degree that if you are not able to humble yourself enough to realize that this particular experience is a "lesson for growth" being handed to you, then you will come "crashing down" to your real reactionary, conditioned, robotic self.

History, and everyday experience is filled with examples of such self-instigated sabotage, which is often viewed as failure.

But it is not failure at all if you realize the gift of the lesson for growth that such an experience presents.

A word to the wise.

---~.~---

5. The Genuine You

How to see yourself more meaningfully.

That would surely be useful, if you are at all serious about your potential and role in life.

Usually we "think" we know how we appear to others.

We judge for ourselves, in our mind (thoughts) how others see us. But, is that an accurate gauge of how you truly appear to others.

The Ancient aphorism "*Know Thyself*" was inscribed in the entrance to the Temple of Apollo at Delphi, in Greece.

Plato employs the maxim 'Know Thyself' extensively pointing out that Socrates is referring to a long-established wisdom. There are at least six Dialogues of Plato which discuss or explore the saying of Delphi: 'Know Thyself.'

Lana and Andy Wachowski (American film directors, screenwriters and producers) used one of the Latin versions (temet nosce) of this aphorism as inscription over the Oracle's door in their movies "**The Matrix**" (1999) **and" The Matrix Revolutions**" (2003).

So, what is this "***Know Thyself***"?

There are different levels to which this saying applies.

At the simplest level the saying "Know Thyself" refers to having an understanding of your relationship to life.

<u>In other words:</u>

How you relate to the world
  (other people, things and ideas);
How you relate to yourself, your thoughts and
  beliefs etc.;

  How do you see yourself?

Do you see yourself through the beliefs that you have acquired?

Do you understand what makes you do the things you do and why you do them?

In other words, do you have a 'handle' on your habits?

There are "higher" or "deeper" levels of understanding the aphorism –

"**Know Thyself**".

This is part of the journey of Mastery of self.

At the deeper levels it deals with comprehending who, or what you actually **are – beyond your body and mind.**

Truth mirrors reality and it logically follows that the best way to decipher the truth about yourself is by personally observing and experiencing the reality of which you are a part.

Utilizing your experience of the world as a reflection (a mirror) of yourself is an important insight.

Seeing yourself as others see you gives a more accurate appraisal of how you "come off" or appear to the world around you.

Other people see you based on their own conditioning and habits. Therefore, they make a judgment of what they "think" you are based on the behavior that they observe and how it affects them.

By carefully observing how others' reactions to you affect your **habitual responses you can learn a lot about the "robotic" nature of your behavior.**

You learn whether there is a "genuine" you interacting with the world.

Or perhaps you will discern to your shock or amazement, that the 'you' that you thought was genuine is actually a fabricated, conditioned response to the various stimuli of the universe which you think you inhabit.

There are many 'levels' or 'degrees' of revelation possible. These all "point to" or "reveal" the depth and richness included in the saying

"**Know Thyself**".

Are thoughts, beliefs and conditioning the ultimate mechanics of who you really are? Are you not <u>much more</u> than such a simplistic mechanistic view of life?

To "Know Thyself" is to discover the GENUINE YOU.

----

6. <u>Watching Thought</u>

One area to explore in personal development and beyond, is how we understand thinking. Is it a tool we use?

Is it what in essence characterizes "the self"?

How does thinking affect our lives, our plans, or is all of that just thought?

The mind is defined by its content. The content of mind is thought. Thus, "no thought – no mind".

This is not necessarily a bad thing, it might be the solution to many of our problems!

The following is from the Introduction of one of my books. Perhaps it will serve a **purpose**

here.

INTRODUCTION

I don't know how to think. DO YOU?

How does one THINK?

Do you squeeze your eyes shut, tighten your entire body and will a thought into being?

What are the mechanics of thought?

Or do thoughts just happen?

Are they just there and over the years we develop an ability to attach to them in some way.

And then do the thoughts become "my thoughts" and "her thoughts" and "their thoughts"?

But if thoughts just happen, then where do they come from?

Some would say that 'you' think.

If that is so, then how would you think to stop thinking?

After all, if you are the one in control of those thoughts you call yours,

then shouldn't you be able to stop them at will?

Go ahead.

Stop thinking.

What will you do?

Shout in your mind "STOP!" or "SHUT UP!".

But those are still thoughts.

That is thinking.

It hasn't stopped.

All of this is happening, and yet someone (something or some nothing) is seeing all this as it happens.

---~.~---

7. **<u>From the "Dao te Ching"</u>**

If you are depressed you are living in the past.

If you are anxious you are living in the future.

If you are at peace you are living in the present. (Lao Tzu)

At a deep level of understanding

You ARE the NOW!

----

8. <u>BEYOND DREAMLAND</u>

WHO AM I ?

I know that I am not my mind (thoughts) nor the body. The mind is a tool I use for interacting with my world of experience.

> The body is a vehicle that enables our third dimensional "dream-world" of experiences.

Both thought (mind) and body have evolved over millennia, through countless experiences.

So here we are.

Are you stuck, thinking that you are nothing more than "body/mind", or maybe "body/mind" and some sort of "intelligence" or intellect?

If that is the case then you are severely limiting your multidimensional expansion into reality.

Step out of "dreamland", taste the reality!

Are you Master of your domain, or

is thought the master of you?

----

9. <u>The Subjective Event</u>

It is widely "assumed" by those who are doing personal development to "develop" themselves in some way, that presumably the goal is to become more effective in a particular area and thus achieve greater success at something.

But, who is this PERSON that
you hope to develop?

Who is this person that you "think" you are?

The <u>PERSON</u> is totally *a subjective event*.

In actuality there is no verifiable objective world "out there". It is all a subjective production and you are the "witness" that is also subjectively present to record or respond to the phenomena perceived by your senses.

Since the human relies on reasoning as the "be-all and end-all", whether it is ultimately true or not, I will attempt to explain the reasoning for the above paragraph. This may "turn on a light" for some readers. Those with an "open mind" for investigation at a "greater depth" will benefit most.

You will be aware that a healthy human is equipped with the so-called five sense organs. These are the five traditionally recognized methods of perception, or sense: sound, sight, touch, smell and taste.

This is the human interface to the so-called "outside" world. Let us take sight (vision) as an example for a deeper look. (pun)

One does not actually "see" through the eyes. The eye is an organ that performs rather similarly to a camera. The lens admits and focuses light rays that are reflected from an object and these rays fall upon the retina where the rods and cones are impressed by the light signal. (Similar to a camera's film or electronic light sensor being impressed by light).

The retina is connected through the optic nerve(s) (synapses etc.), which carries the electrochemical signal to the visual cortex of the brain, which incidentally, is at the BACK of the brain (whereas the eyes are at the front of the brain).

So far, this is the simplest of scientific/medical explanations for the sense of sight.

However, if we look a little closer with some real investigative curiosity, we might ask: "So do I, or does the brain actually see a tree that I might be looking at?"

That is a great question! We assume that we "see" what we are "looking at", but is that really so. This may be a simple basic way of communicating the event, but how do we know in actuality that we are "seeing" at tree?

All that the brain receives at the visual cortex is a signal (electrochemical or electro-magnetic) and the signal has no resemblance to an actual tree.

It seems that we humans experience a visual event and then draw upon inherent organic experience (cellular memory perhaps) to gain a perception of some sort about the signals that come to us through the eyes.

Over the evolutionary period of the human species a consensus in the collective consciousness of mankind has brought about agreement about our experiences with the so-called outside world.

The entire conceptualization of this "outside world" is resident in memory or thought, as a conclusion or assumption based on millennia of agreed-upon definitions of perception by the 5 senses. It is all subjective.

Even to measure such "outside" events through humanly conceived instrumentation is not conclusive of an actual outside world. The interpretation is still subjective, as it is processed by our conceptual "mind" system.

If one looks very deeply, very hesitantly, without the burden of all the preconceived and formulated "knowledge" of mankind, one might see that:

THE WORLD IS WITHIN YOU!

This has been the perennial understanding of the great spiritual traditions and ancient mystery schools.

Science is just beginning to touch upon some of this mystery through areas such as quantum mechanics and trans-personal psychology.

If you are really interested to find out more about yourself, then do not rely on the authority of "others" to condition your thinking.
= Escape the MATRIX.=

Be the Master. Mastery of self is the first step to everything, and – "the first step is the last step" from the following quote:

The first step is the last step

... The first step is the last step. The first step is to perceive, perceive what you are thinking, perceive your ambition, perceive your anxiety, your loneliness, your despair, this extraordinary sense of sorrow, perceive it, without any condemnation, justification, without wishing it to be different. Just to perceive it, as it is. When you perceive it as it is, then there is a totally different kind of action taking place, and that action is the final action. ...

- J. Krishnamurti

10.

Light of Joy

You are a child of freedom,
And yet you give it up so quickly -

And then the light of day
is longer in coming.

As a babe, not long out of the light,
In the depth of your eyes,
gleamed a spark sublime.

And the world wanted your joy.

But the burden of the world,
Could not understand the light of joy,

And failed to see its worth.

-wladicus

------ ~.~ ------

11. <u>The Defensive Mechanism</u>

In the early days of the human species the survival instinct was very strong. This is necessary for the survival of any species. In the case of humans, like most other animals, it took the form of "fight or flight".

The human consciousness and energy within the body was always in a state of alertness, ready to defend the body from injury or to run away from imminent and lethal danger.

Now, we live in a fairly secure environment where the necessity for physical survival is not as prevalent as it used to be. Humans have evolved a superior mental capacity that has improved the chances of survival of the species to a large degree from the physical perspective.

However, the "fight or flight" instinct has not disappeared. It has shifted to the environment of the psyche.

The human of today, to a great extent, lives in "the head", in ideas and concepts, and projected images of what should and shouldn't be.

This tendency to dwell under the influence of "mind" (i.e. the thought realm) creates a virtual world for the psyche.

It is in the realm of the psyche where the survival instinct has now found a new arena for renewed, activity.

Defending one's self-image, opinions, etc., has become the number one priority of the "fight or flight" instinct. It is still there for protecting from possible physical dangers, but a bit more sluggish in that area.

In the psyche this instinct has transmuted into a "defense" mechanism. Its priority is the defend what you think you are, your perceived value, your "rightness" or your "rights", your opinion.

The attitude of mind has degenerated to a state of "me above everyone else". This attitude was necessary for the early survival of the species when the intellect was not as "highly" developed as it is today, but it no longer serves the human species when we are looking for harmonious ways to live together and survive without destroying ourselves through mental instabilities.

Now, more than ever before, we need to master the mind which is capable of forging many different kinds of instabilities and survival problems for the species.

Mastery of self is an approach that works. We must be masters of the thought realm that has brought us to our current technical heights, but is now also testing our very sanity under the disguise of fulfilling various desires.

The next time you spot the "defensive" mechanism arising to protect your position, opinion, belief, or whatever mental or intellectual category – **STOP** – for a moment, and notice that the very words coming out of your mouth, or the reactive thoughts just beginning to explode into words, are the potentially lethal weapons that can create great disharmony and unneeded turmoil in your, and others' life experience.

Can you rise above your conditioned limitations?

Are you a Master of self?

Begin now, if you haven't already.

You can only add to the next evolutionary

improvement of self and humanity.

---~.~---

12. **PLAY the GAME!**

Life is the grandest game that you can play. It is the game of games, the basis for the conceived and the conceivable.

In a very real sense, LIFE is what you ARE. But that may be too quick a jump for some people to grasp. So look at it as a game.

In essence, you are the game. You determine how you will play it. There is one important detail that must be understood first. The Rules.

Are there Rules to the "Game of Life"?

Well, we might call them "Conditions" or "Understandings". The interesting thing is that you are the holder of those understandings or conditions. They emanate from the source of your being.

This "Game of Life" is designed for you to experience various phenomena. In a certain way of speaking, you have put yourself into a scenario similar to that in the movie "*MATRIX*".

Because we need a concept of some sort to communicate an idea, I say "similar" to the movie MATRIX, but not the same.

This game is possible, because in from a certain point of view you have put yourself (i.e. your true BEINGness) to sleep so that you can experience a pseudo reality of a world through the medium of mind (which is thought).

In this "game" (played in the field of a "dream"), you have forgotten your true source and nature by choice, so that you can experience the life that you *are* from many different aspects.

Your interface for experiencing is the human body with the traditional senses of sight, smell, touch, hearing and taste.

The stimulus coming via these five senses reach the brain where the incoming sensory signals are interpreted and acted upon or reacted to, depending on your level of focus of attention – through the awareness that you are.

Consciousness is a facet of the awareness. Consciousness is the field of energy within which your world of experience, including the body and mind, manifest.

Your "mission" in this game of life, should you choose to accept it, is to learn from the experiences that you "go through" (that is what experience literally means -"to go through").

The "learning" is not a memorizing of facts like in school, but a kind of "remembering" of who you really are. Through these experiences of life you gain Mastery of self (i.e. understanding how the 'self' of the game is NOT the Self that you really are).

In other words you "learn" that what is going on in the mind is not who you are and has no control over your destiny unless you are still asleep to reality.

By promoting a singly focused attitude to discern the actual or 'real' from the ephemeral throughout the course of the game of life you start removing the 'blockages' or the 'veil' that covers the 'truth of what actually is".

Thus you begin to "awaken from the dream" of the life that you project through a personally conceived world that appears to be full of contradictions, problems and suffering in general. From a personal point of view that will all change when you awaken from the dream.

Mastery of self is the road to the discovery of the "Kingdom of Heaven" or the "Kingdom of Happiness" WITHIN THE REAL YOU.

These are only words and thoughts, a limited method available to us to communicate something of the reality we seek to understand. However, words are

sometimes effective when they can carry the energy of a metaphor, or parable, or some poetic verse to communicate a deeper understanding than thought could ever manage.

---~.~---

13. <u>The Day the World Stood Still</u>

Each of us lives in a world that is unique to our perception. One might say that in a strange way, we see what we expect to see, what our conditioning and preconceived notions make us believe we see.

That is why sometimes we cannot agree exactly on what we

> **- see, saw**
> **__or__ *think***
> **we__see or saw.**

There is, of course, a collective consensus of human consciousness that sort of sets the background ideas and beliefs upon which we all agree, or use as a foundation upon which we 'build' our personal 'world'.

So, in many ways by this consensus of consciousness, we all appear to live in and see a very similar world, that we have 'bought into' to 'protect' ourselves from deeply ingrained personal feelings of insecurity.

This reliance of the foundation of a consensus consciousness allays many of the fears that might otherwise push us closer to more insane behavior.

We feel the security of a larger group of people that share a similar foundation of beliefs.

This is the only common element in 'seeing' a world to appear to be the same or similar for everyone who is part of the collective.

However, in the seclusion of our 'personal' minds (thoughts) we can still feel totally separate and lonely whenever the collective concepts or beliefs of the world fail to meet our needs or our personal vision of what the world should be.

Some of us are courageous enough to question the very thinking that has conditioned us, that has given us our beliefs and our basic sense of security in the world.

Some of us have refused to "march to the same drummer". We question the reality of those very assumptions and beliefs that have promised much, but have failed to produce a deep sense of security.

No matter what you "believe" it still does not seem to change social behavior or take away the fears of aggression, wars, or unfair treatment.

Will such things as Personal Development really lead you to freedom? Even if you meticulously practice the teachings of such offerings, and do achieve a modicum of success, will you have found freedom and joy?

There are countless stories of those who have acquired those 'heights', have delighted and bathed in those riches and still came crashing down and learned the illusory power of beliefs that promise to make something of you that is really not possible.

The only way any work on yourself will lead to some great discoveries and maybe even a marvelous transformation, is by some deep self enquiry. In a sense you must find out what really "makes you tick"; why you are the way you are.

Is what you fancy yourself to be, or to become, a viable growth strategy?

Mastery of self has been taught by all the great teachers this world has known. None of them promised to make a better you.

They all pointed to the fact that you have veiled your ability to see and to understand with various inhibiting beliefs and degenerative ideas. They asked you to meet the challenge of being "true to yourself".

The "better" you is already there, but you are blind to the uncovering of it.

You see the world "out there" a certain way. But it is really the world "in there" – within you, conditioned by your beliefs, your thinking that creates the illusory world you struggle in, find fault with, and try to overcome.

Can you make that world within stand still, just for a moment? – –

Long enough to see that it is the image built of your desires and shortcomings?

If you can take this challenge, and muster just enough courage to question the very substance of that illusory world, then you can transform it.

YOU are the only one who can make
THAT world release its hold on you.

Yes, _YOU_ can transform your world!

Through Mastery of self you can move the
"mountains" of your inner world to forge a
brave new world that is a reflection of a deep
integrity of life. But even in a very practical
way, you can affect the change in the course of
your destiny by your choosing to be Master
over mind.

You may come to really know yourself for the
first time on the day you make the 'WORLD'
STAND STILL.

---~.~---

14. <u>I Heard There Was A Secret Chord</u>

The first line from Leonard Cohen's "Hallelujah" stirs the spirit and 'plucks heart-strings'.

Speechless, one can only say "Hallelujah", and it says everything! The mind cannot decode this.

The mind can hypothesize, and imagine many things, but when the "spirit" and "heart" move in full vibrancy, the mind is dumbfounded. It can only "babble".

Where are YOU when this happens? Who are you? What are you?

This "stunning of the mind", is like the blast of bright sunlight that hits your eyes when you quickly throw open heavy window curtains. *The "heavy curtains of inhibiting concepts" have suddenly parted transporting "you" into <u>non-local</u> reality.*

In that instant of non-local disorientation, where is the "personal" you? Your mind/thoughts, self-image, opinions about who you are etc. are incapable of entering the dimension beyond mind.

That "you", the "personal" you, the self-image you, is a construct of mind. This mental construct is a limited ephemeral image that is always changing and has no concrete substance.

That YOU that you *'think' you are*, had a beginning and will come to an end when the body/brain/mind pass away.

But, there is a YOU that is not bound by the limitations of body/mind. That YOU, knows that it exists.

The body/mind "you", the "you" that you normally think of when you refer to yourself, your ideas, your feelings, your plans, your desires, your fears, etc., that "you" is constantly changing.

The body/mind you once had a baby's body; next this "you" was associated with the feelings and body of a school youngster; a later "you" became a teenager – then the adult "you" appeared.

Which "you" was the real you and not a conceptual mental image-based "you"?

Through all those "life experiences" of "you" there was a steadfast, consistent YOU that was there "witnessing" all those characters that you thought/ believed were "you".

Begin with small steps, with the little things of everyday experience.

◊   Observe the activity of mind, the thoughts that cross your attention.

◊   Notice how certain thoughts 'grab' your attention in such a way that you feel helpless in reacting to the demands and stimuli affecting body and mind.

◊ Become a "witness." A dispassionate witness. Do not get involved in the thoughts parading before your awareness. Do not give them your attention.

◊ Just watch them with curiosity. These thoughts cannot harm you, they cannot move you to do anything undesirable – unless you let them.

These are the initial steps to Mastery of self. That "self" that is the image of the mind. Go slowly, gradually. Note that you cannot really define the real YOU which is not of the mind. That YOU might be labeled as the "Self" as opposed to the "self" of the mind.

As you begin to be Master of self, the greater Self has more and more opportunities to guide you through life experiences.

There will be a lessening of inner conflict and turmoil. You are on the road to the peace.

Not peace from something, but the peace that you naturally are.

Mastery of self is the road to freedom – not freedom from something, but freedom itself, which is a state of being rather than a condition.

**And then perhaps you might say
that you "heard a secret chord"
that the "holy spirit" played
on your "heart-strings".**

Hallelujah

---~.~---

15. <u>Non-personal criticism</u>

Although criticism of a "person" is never valid, those people who insist on doing it are really trying to bring attention to themselves. Tacitly, their psyche is seeking approval from others. They need confirmation of their value, that people should notice them.

The most basic way of explaining this is that there is a lack of love.

Maybe not so obvious, but quite sound if one looks deeply enough, giving love invites love and thus no lack is felt.

However, this is not so easily seen by the 'soul' crying out for attention and thus striking out at the 'world' expressing anger, disagreement and in general, finding fault with others.

Criticizing *a "person" is never valid!*

If it is one's function to oversee, supervise or teach, then analytical appraisal of how things should be done correctly can fall under the caption of "constructive criticism".

It is basically unkind to make the "person" themselves the subject of criticism of any kind.

Clearly explained, task-related evaluation is often a useful sort of "constructive" criticism.

In such cases the person receiving the task-related criticism will usually understand that it is not a personal attack (unless the person lacks an appropriate degree of maturity to cope with such a situation).

And yet, it appears that a sizable part of society is often willing to launch attacks on "persons" and their characters (personal attacks).

By deeply looking within oneself, one might see with some compassion that many people are coping with a growing process or a maturation process, that is as yet incomplete. Thus we witness the manifestation of undesirable behavior.

Many of us have either gone through something similar, or are still going through this growth to understand what life is all about.

By our compassionate and understanding behavior in the presence of **personal criticism we empower another towards maturation by example.**

If, for a few moments, we can look beyond our self-focused mentality then we might 'see' that we actually are one big family (of sorts).

All humans are at the root, very similar in disposition regarding their own safety and fulfillment of personal desires.

Everyone is seeking approval or recognition in some form or other. No-one wants to feel lonely and separate from others, and yet we find that the 'ego' to a large degree sabotage our ability to 'connect' with others by putting on "airs of superiority" or by expressing disgust, or fear of the other (anthrop phobia).

Criticism has become a favorite 'tool' of the 'ego' in maintaining its self importance. Although this may make a person 'feel good' for a while, criticism has the characteristic energy of negative "lash back" in the form of "Judge not lest ye be judged".

When you judge another you are always, in every case, judging yourself. This is an obvious observation if you look at it very closely. You can only see in another that which is already part of your own consciousness.

So, if you see a particular annoying behavior in another, you can be certain that you either have experienced something of a similar nature, or you currently have some similar habit as part of your character, but have not noticed it yet.

The urge to judge another is a 'hint' of sorts to look at yourself first.

("First remove the log in your own eye,
then you can remove the splinter
in your brother's eye").

Compassion is always the mark of a human being that is considerate and focused on finding out how he or she truly "fits into" the universe.

---~.~---

16. <u>THE ENDING OF TIME</u>

"Time, oh time,

Where did you go?"

– from Michael Merchant's song "TIME"

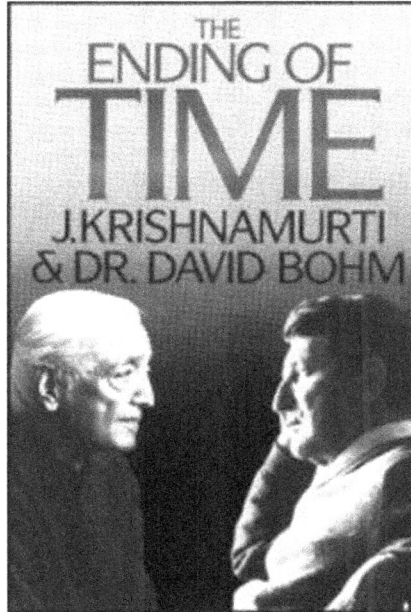

Physicist Dr. David Bohm had several talks with the renowned master of intellectual/spiritual dialogue J. Krishnamurti.

The in-depth dialogue was about time as it is seen and understood from many different levels and aspects.

As a physicist, Dr. Bohm wanted to know how a scientific/intellectual understanding of time related to our understanding of life.

This dialogue reached far beyond any expected intellectual ideations.

To his surprise, through the process of dialogue with J. Krishnamurti, Dr. Bohm discovered that the deeper levels of scientific understanding of time were beginning to reach far beyond the outdated scientific understandings that existed before quantum theory established a foothold in scientific thought.

The exchange between Dr. Bohm and J. Krishnamurti extended to a total of 13 dialogues which were all recorded and then transcribed into book form under the title "The Ending of Time" was published in 1985.

It became quite clear that the concept of time is a useful unit of measurement, like the inch, yard, or ounce in practical areas of application.

Scientific calculations, contract terms, appointment and meeting schedules, etc. are useful applications of the concept of time.

However, when one includes time in their belief system where time acquires meanings beyond practical conceptual applications, then various conundrums and calamities begin to invade and contaminate one's understanding of life.

When the psyche gets attached to a certain idea of time it can cause psychological distortions of all sorts in the way one relates to the world and oneself.

A fixed idea of time introduces limitations that can shape one's beliefs and mislead one's approach to living life in a more auspicious manner.

Ideas of past, present, and future, have their practical place; but when they lead to neurosis and fear of what will happen in the future and so on, then we begin to see the far-reaching misunderstanding of this thing we call 'time'.

What is your understanding of time?

Does time rule your life, or have you mastered this tricky concept as it relates to your daily life?

How do you understand the ending of time?

---~.~---

17. Identity

If you wish to continue to "develop the PERSON" as in "Personal Development" then please continue, for that is the clearest way that you can see and understand at this moment of your life experience.

However, there is a "secret" that few have understood.

It is not really a secret.

It only appears to be a secret because we have blocked or covered up access to it by our own limiting concepts of identity. (Here we are not discussing identity in the legal sense).

"Personal" identity is a by-product of imagination and thought.

Your true identity supersedes both thought and imagination.

All the great sages have taught this throughout recorded history and even before: But only a very few have understood the teachings.

Most people who hear the teachings think that the teachings apply to the betterment and growth of the "person".

On one level this may be true to a degree, but it is not permanent.

PERSON or person-hood is a psychological identity.

"Personal" identity is a derivative of thought.

This identity is easily affected by all sorts of circumstances which are conceptually related. Personal identity, being sourced from thought, is impermanent, unstable and susceptible to the ever-changing "whims of thought". It is only an ephemeral identity.

Mastery of self is one approach to "drawing back the veil" that covers this mystery. Your true identity begins to reveal itself as your conditioned habits of thought and behavior are understood for what they are.

You are the silent witness.

---~.~---

18. Being Authentic

When you have a question that arises from your deep desire to truly understand your current confusion then it is often very helpful to enter a state of calm and look at the question itself and the possible reason that it has arisen.

With a little care you will see the answer, or at least an indication, or a sign that in essence points you towards the discovery of a meaningful answer. The answer need not necessarily be in the form of words or thoughts. Often just a feeling of knowingness provides comforting assurance.

Whenever you find yourself in a situation where it becomes necessary to comment on something that may be offensive or disturbing to others, know that from a place of authenticity of BEING it can be done with skill, finesse and attentiveness to delivering the comment(s) in the kindest way possible.

Even if your answer or commenting seem to be unappreciated remain authentic and true to the deepest sense of your true self.

There is no need to feel that you have "won" or made your point.

Debate is OK if that is the state of your mind, however, loftier and more constructive states are a nobler aim.

This is exemplary of success in a most auspicious form.

As to being critical of others - earlier in this book I wrote:

> Criticizing a "person" is never valid!
>
> If it is one's function to oversee, supervise or teach, then analytical
>
> appraisal of how things should be done correctly can fall under the caption of "constructive criticism".

In all cases, be considerate of others, and allow compassion and understanding to be your guide in human relations -

"To thine own self be true..."

There is a deep subtlety to the whole idea of criticism.

We are ALWAYS judging ourselves.
- Until we stop doing it to others.

As the saying goes "What goes around comes around".

The older version is "As you sow, so shall you reap".

This is a self revealing experience attested to by many.

Most of what comes from mind itself is simply opinion, which can be viewed as a natural "perpetual motion machine".

You are the witness who can bring order to thought through vigilant attention and focus of consciousness.

This is part of Mastery of self and being authentic.

The statement made above:

"To thine own self be true..."

Relates to "Mastery of self"

The key is to be master of the habitual self to free the expressions of the "higher or intuitive

" Self that is at the core of one's being.

I see Shakespeare's "**Thine own self**" as the true Self, and not the conditioned, troubled self.

The habitual self is a product of conditioning, limiting beliefs and falsely understood identity. It is the reactive, fearful and survival-focused remnant of the primitive human of past millennia.

This primitive nature of mankind has dominated most of humanity's thinking to such a degree that an insightful or intuitive understanding of life has become virtually impossible.

Fantasies, theories, limiting beliefs and often uncontrolled emotional behavior continue to captivate people in sort of a dream state, a pseudo reality, where life's dramas play themselves out, often on a stage of sorrow.

Even a truly auspicious reasoning capability has been hampered by the intrusion of this "conditioned mind" which continues to disturb our peace and sanity in a variety of compelling ways.

Some conditioning is necessary. But when it subdues our creative nature, true expression of BEING and authenticity, then we must awaken from that limiting dream.

It is the dream of the false self that believes that the dream of mentation is reality.

> This is the "self" of the mind.
> The conditioned self.
> The limited self.
> The fearful self.
> The guilt-ridden self.
> The confused self.
> The hopeful and hopeless self.

"To thine own self be true..."

That is the non-conditioned, not habitual, not limited, not bound or enslaved self.

It is this Self to which one should be true

> (I see this as the deepest interpretation)

One might call it the "Spiritual" self or the "true" self.

Those are only words but I use them just to make a distinction in a different direction.

The habitual self that most everyone is aware of as "themselves" is the body/mind identity self.

The self identity which is focused on the body/mind experience as reality, is a mere by-product of thought processes.

To see it, know it and understand it as only a character of your worldly experiences is a move towards your total freedom from the limiting conditioning of thought and the resulting habits that bind one to a limited expression of life.

You are much more than the imaginings of mind.

The "bettering" of that limited self gets you nowhere in the end, because the personal body/mind passes on but the "core being Self" which was there even before your birth has never changed. It has always been present,

The "Real You" has always been present, but this has gone unnoticed because of the strong habitual attachment and belief in the body/mind as reality.

You, are already complete and need no "improvement".

The BEINGness that you are is part of the impersonal nature, of creation - the universe - reality - whatever way it might be described, therefore personal development does not apply to this Self that you are.

Once you have acquired a Mastery of self then you can "play" your role of "worldly" self with greater understanding and usefulness to world that others inhabit. You have left the MATRIX of limitations and are truly free. You can help to awaken others that are ready to listen.

But first, take a closer look at what Mastery of self entails for you.

Of course, you do not have to accept any of this, and that is perfectly alright. That is the basic freedom that all humans have, the freedom to choose.

You make the choice.

Perhaps you could give

Mastery of Self

-a closer look -

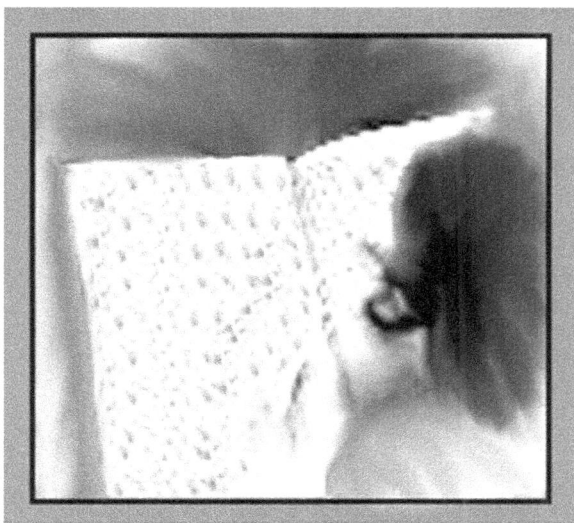

----- ~.~ -----

Walter Dutchak

ABOUT THE AUTHOR

Walter Dutchak has had a varied career, and eclectic education. His interests vary over a large range including music (playing classical guitar, violin and CDs), art (painting a bit), amateur astronomy, philosophy, spiritual topics, and chess.

His career has included teaching school children and adults, writing technical courses, engineering technology, computer programming and application design and about 22 years in the communications industry.

Main current interests include self inquiry and understanding relationships in their variety of manifestations. He has studied authors such as Eckhart Tolle and keeps in touch with the many satsung sessions that are recorded by various "spiritual" teachers as found on You Tube.

In the past two years Walter has written 4 books:

Thoughts and Time,
Watching Thought,
Mastery of Self – an inquiry
 and the current book
Mastery of Self – a closer look.

www.ingramcontent.com/pod-product-compliance
Lightning Source LLC
Chambersburg PA
CBHW032040040426
42449CB00007B/965